Meadowlark was Afraid of the Dark

Written by PJ Kelly

Art by YoungJu Kim

ISBN: 978-1-63901-650-1

FIRST EDITION

To Veera...The Spark!

In a beautiful patch of Atlantic,
Swam a toothy, ginormous beast,
Fish darted around him, quite frantic,
When they feared he was ready to feast.

His movements were stealthy and steady,
Making others believe he was slow.
With a flash of a fin he was ready,
To devour any morsel below.

Unlike his undersea neighbors,
He never hunted at night,
A very peculiar behavior
For a perpetually hungry Great White.

Deep down he felt whatchamacallits,
That topsy-turvied within,
More powerful than his pulsing gills,
Scarier than his zig-zaggy grin.

Despite being both fearsome and fearful,
With a bite so much worse than his bark,
He hid an embarrassing secret...

Meadowlark was afraid of the dark!

It bothered him more than a little,
That he bore such a fanciful name,
But to watch the sun fade and to be so afraid,
Left him confused and trembling with shame.

He always always swam close to the surface,
When the moon was bright......well, alright!
But if dark, misty haze obscured lunar rays,
Meadow braced for a very long night.

Each day he held his terror inside,
As he powered his way through the ocean,
Whipping his tail and gnashing his teeth,
He was able to control his emotion.

Finally one night, a storm so severe,
Made the ocean churn upside down,

The rain was insane, the thunder he feared,
Would erupt and drown out all sound.

Meadow plunged in a panic into the abyss,
Past mackerel and albacore too,
Chased by a fear he couldn't resist,

Darker
    and
        darker it grew.

Suddenly solo, he peered left and right,
The deep was much blacker than blue,

"Oh noooo," he groaned, completely alone,
He couldn't decide what to do!

Wait!

Was that light that he spied up ahead?

How could that possibly be?

His tail pushed him forward, mostly with dread,

Miles down under the sea.

A bright beacon beckoned—what a relief!

But attached was a VERY strange creature,

A roly-poly body with toothpick-like teeth,

A mishmash of contrasting features.

"SALUTATIONS!" said the fellow,

with barely a move,

His mouth covering all of his face.

His body swayed smoothly to an internal groove,

while his lantern remained firmly in place.

"My name is Bojangles, I'm an angler fish.

That light on my head? Doesn't come with a switch.

It's on all the time, to show off my smile...

Bet you haven't seen choppers like these in a while!"

A curious sight, this fish with a light,
And a name that was quirky and kind,
Warm luminescence revealed his real essence,

Bojangles—a lifesaving find!

Meadowlark was instantly soothed by bright Bo,
And laughed at his silly routine,
With his novel night-light, he felt suddenly right
At home in the aqua marine.

They chatted for days about oceanic ways,
And shared their undersea fears.

They realized in a hurry,
that EVERYONE worries,

But eventually,
EVERY storm clears.

They became fast friends, swam for hours on end,
Never thought twice about night,
Because Bo was aglow with an energy flow,
That was powered by nonstop delight.

One day, Meadowlark made a happy remark,
"Hallelujah! I'm over my fright!"

"Night is quite nice, and it's better by twice,
With Bo, it's a swim in the park!"

Onward they went, with all their time spent,
Between the surface and the way-way-down deep,
And at the end of the day,
when the sun went away,

Meadowlark enjoyed a peaceful shark sleep.

Now...

In a beautiful patch of Atlantic,
Swims a toothy, ginormous beast.
Fish darting around him in circles,

With nothing to fear in the least!

Glossary

Underwater Words:

abyss: a vast pit, too deep to be measured

albacore: a type of tuna that can also be called a longfin or white tuna

angler fish: a type of fish that lives deep in the ocean. It finds food with a light that comes off the front of its head, which acts like a fishing lure.

Atlantic: the world's second largest ocean and covers 25% of the Earth's surface

aqua marine: a fancy way to say marine water or ocean

mackerel: fish that live in the Atlantic Ocean

Glossary

Nonsense (Silly) Words:

mishmash: a jumbled mess; hodgepodge

roly-poly: short and plump; pudgy

salutations: a way to greet someone or say
Hello.

topsy-turvied: upside down

whatchamacallits: something whose name
is unknown or forgotten

zig-zaggy: a line or course that moves back
and forth to form a series of sharp angles.